Unfolding
Grace

STUDY GUIDE

Unfolding Grace

STUDY GUIDE

A Guided Study through the Bible

CROSSWAY®

WHEATON, ILLINOIS

Crossway is a publishing ministry of Good News Publishers.

RRDS	31	30	29	28	27	26	25	24	23	22	21
13	12	11	10	9	8	7	6	5	4	3	2

CONTENTS

INTRODUCTION

to the *Unfolding Grace Study Guide*

The *Unfolding Grace Study Guide* is designed to be used in conjunction with *Unfolding Grace: 40 Guided Readings through the Bible*. This study guide offers

1. a brief summary for each of the seven parts of *Unfolding Grace*, drawing together the main themes of each part's readings;
2. multiple questions for each of the 40 guided readings in *Unfolding Grace*. These questions are designed to lead readers into deeper reflection on the ways God's plan of redemption unfolds across each reading; and
3. closing questions at the end of each of the seven parts, which assist readers in considering more richly that part in its entirety.

As you explore these summaries and questions in individual and/or small group settings, our prayer is that this *Unfolding Grace Study Guide* would expand your appreciation for God's redemption in Christ as it develops across the pages of Scripture.

Part 1

THE STORY BEGINS

God creates a good world and fills it with communal life. He makes humanity in his image to know him and reflect his character and rule. But Adam and Eve shatter the peace of Eden through their sinful rejection of God. The Lord rightly responds with just judgment: man is sent out of God's presence in Eden, living exiled from his true home with God and then eventually returning to dust in death. Yet God uses this now fallen world to display his infinite mercy through the story of redemption that follows. He promises to send a descendant of Eve, a Savior, to conquer the Evil One and restore the lost blessings of Eden to mankind.

God judges the world with a flood, yet he graciously preserves Noah and his family so that God might continue to unfold his promises to renew the world. The Lord then chooses to bless one man—Abraham—as the means of blessing for all peoples. In generation after generation God overcomes obstacles to ensure that his promise safely passes from Abraham to Isaac and to Jacob and to

Jacob's twelve sons. Even though these sons betray their brother Joseph by selling him into slavery, the Lord blesses Joseph and uses him to preserve his family when they move to Egypt in the midst of a famine.

1. GOD'S CREATION AND HUMANITY'S FALL
Genesis 1–4

What does God originally create the world to be like, and how does this shape our expectation for what he plans the world's eternal future to be like?

_____

_____

_____

_____

What effects of Adam's first sin do we all continue to experience today?

_____

_____

_____

_____

What key promise does God make to humanity after the fall? How do Jesus' cross and resurrection decisively fulfill this promise?

---

2. THE FLOOD AND GOD'S COVENANT WITH NOAH
Genesis 6–9

What does the judgment of the flood teach us about humanity's character and God's?

After the flood, what does God promise to Noah and to creation? Why is this important for the story of redemption?

---

3. BABEL AND THE PROMISE TO ABRAHAM
Genesis 10–12

What does the story of Babel teach us about mankind's values and priorities?

_____

_____

_____

_____

_____

_____

_____

What three major promises does God make to Abraham?

_____

_____

_____

_____

_____

_____

4. ABRAHAM AND THE PROMISE OF ISAAC

Genesis 15–18

What does Abraham's life teach us about the nature of true faith?

How does God intentionally cultivate Abraham's faith in these chapters?

How are we, like Abraham and Sarah, tempted to doubt God and his promises today?

5. THE PROMISE TO ISAAC AND THE BLESSING OF JACOB

Genesis 25–28

What obstacles do God's promises to Abraham face in these chapters?

_____

_____

_____

_____

_____

_____

How does God overcome these obstacles? What does this reveal about his character?

_____

_____

_____

_____

_____

_____

6. ISRAEL COMES TO EGYPT

Genesis 45–48

How do we see the Lord working in the life of Joseph? How can this encourage us in our own suffering?

How does the story of Joseph's provision for his family relate to the unfolding of God's three promises to Abraham?

CLOSING QUESTIONS

What major themes have you discovered in the book of Genesis?

_____

_____

_____

_____

_____

How has your view of God been clarified through reflecting on these passages and their development of the big storyline of the Bible and history?

_____

_____

_____

_____

_____

How should your life be impacted as a result of these reflections?

_____

_____

_____

_____

_____

Part 2

GOD'S PEOPLE REDEEMED

God multiplies the Israelites while they are in Egypt. Yet, while the people of Israel grow in number, they also cry out because of their slavery to the Egyptians. God chooses to deliver them by raising up Moses as their leader. After a series of judgments on Egypt, God leads his people out from Egypt through the Red Sea. He then brings them to the foot of Mount Sinai in order to enter into a covenant relationship with them. Israel is to become a new humanity, a kingdom of priests restored to God and reflecting his character in the world. God also causes his presence to dwell with his people in the tabernacle. He brings them out of slavery in order to bring them near to him; he delivers them in order to dwell with them.

From Sinai, God will lead his people to their new home, the land of Canaan. However, Israel continually distrusts and disobeys the Lord. Because of this, God causes them to wander in the wilderness for forty years until this first generation passes away. The next generation will be another fresh start, and God leads them into the land through Joshua, their new Moses-like leader.

7. ISRAEL'S OPPRESSION AND MOSES' CALL

Exodus 1–3

What does God's rescue of Israel teach us about his heart and character?

_____

_____

_____

_____

_____

How does God's rescue of Israel relate to his promises to Abraham in Genesis? What does this teach us about the motivations of God's heart to rescue his people through Jesus?

_____

_____

_____

_____

_____

_____

8. GOD'S JUDGMENT OF EGYPT
Exodus 7–10

God judged Egypt so that the world would know who he is and what he is like. Therefore, what do we learn about him from this section?

How do we see God's sovereignty and human responsibility working together in Pharaoh's life?

9. GOD'S DELIVERANCE OF ISRAEL

Exodus 12–15

What is the purpose of the Passover meal? How does it point forward to the work of Christ for his people?

_____

_____

_____

_____

_____

How does God's deliverance of Israel foreshadow his gracious salvation of people through Jesus?

_____

_____

_____

_____

What do we learn about God—who he is and what he does—from Israel's song on the shore of the Red Sea?

_____

_____

_____

10. GOD'S COVENANT WITH ISRAEL
Exodus 18–20

What does God's statement that "You shall be to me a kingdom of priests and a holy nation" mean for the way in which Israel is to understand its identity and mission?

Since God saved his people and *then* gave them commandments (he did not say, "Obey me and then I will rescue you"), how should God's grace motivate his people to obey him moment by moment?

What do God's various laws to Israel reveal about God's values and the priorities he desires his people to embrace?

_____

_____

_____

_____

11. THE IDOLATRY OF ISRAEL AND THE HEART OF GOD
Exodus 32–34

What does God reveal to Moses about his character, and how does this give great hope to even the worst of sinners?

_____

_____

_____

_____

What does Moses' plea for the Lord to go with his people teach us about what is most valuable in life?

_____

_____

_____

How does the crucifixion of Jesus ultimately resolve the apparent tension in these chapters between God's mercy to sinners and the upholding of his justice?

12. ISRAEL'S JOURNEY AND REBELLION

Numbers 10–14

What are several ways in which these chapters demonstrate different aspects of the nature of sin?

What does this section teach us about why complaining and grumbling in life is a significant spiritual problem?

_____

_____

_____

_____

_____

13. ISRAEL ENTERS THE LAND
Joshua 1–4

How is Joshua presented as a new Moses?

_____

_____

_____

_____

What similarities exist between the story of the exodus and this narrative of Israel's entering the land?

_____

_____

_____

_____

CLOSING QUESTIONS

What are you learning about the human condition from the biblical story-line so far, and how do you see this condition reflected in your own heart?

What are you learning about God's purposes for human history?

How should your life be changed as a result of what you are learning about God and his purposes for his people?

Part 3

GOD'S KINGDOM ESTABLISHED

God brings the people of Israel into the land of Canaan through Joshua's leadership. In doing so, he continues to fulfill his promises to Abraham: he multiplies Abraham's offspring and gives them this good land to inhabit. But Israel rejects God and slides into a spiritual, moral, political, and social decline. In response, God graciously brings order to the nation by giving Saul as its first king. But when Saul proves to be prideful and unfaithful to the Lord, God gives his people David, a flawed but humble king.

God promises David that his line will never end—his lineage will lead to an eternal kingdom. God will channel the blessings of Abraham through the line of David (ultimately leading to Jesus). David's son Solomon builds a temple for God's presence and brings Israel into its greatest time of material blessing.

14. ISRAEL'S CYCLE OF SIN AND RESTORATION

Judges 1–4

In what ways does Israel fail to obey the Lord?

How does this section show us God's patience toward his people?

What aspect of the story of Jael and Sisera echoes God's first gospel promise, spoken to the Serpent: "I will put enmity between you and the woman, and between your offspring and her offspring; he shall bruise your head, and you shall bruise his heel"?

_____

_____

_____

15. ISRAEL NEEDS A KING

Judges 17–21

A refrain of this section is "Everyone did what was right in his own eyes."
How does this section reveal the consequences of embracing this kind of
moral relativism?

_____

_____

_____

_____

_____

Where do we see the effects of moral relativism today?

_____

_____

_____

_____

_____

16. ISRAEL RECEIVES A KING

1 Samuel 7–11

Even though God long promised to provide a king for Israel, what is wrong with Israel's request for a king in this narrative?

How do we see God's sovereignty in even the smallest details of the story of Saul, and how can this comfort us in our everyday lives?

17. THE REJECTION OF SAUL AND ANOINTING OF DAVID

1 Samuel 15–17

What does God's rejection of Saul teach us about how God views sin?

What does the story of David's anointing teach us about the character qualities that God values most? How do we see these embodied in Jesus?

How does David's defeat of Goliath foreshadow Jesus' work on behalf of his people?

18. THE COVENANT WITH DAVID

2 Samuel 5–8

What is the central promise that God makes to David concerning David's descendants?

How does Jesus ultimately fulfill this promise to David?

19. THE KINGDOM ESTABLISHED THROUGH SOLOMON

1 Kings 1–4

Where in this section do you hear echoes of God's central kingdom promises to David and his descendants?

How do we see God working and fulfilling his promises throughout this section?

20. THE TEMPLE BUILT BY SOLOMON
1 Kings 6–9

What are the key purposes of the temple for God's people?

What does Solomon's prayer teach us about prayer and the kinds of requests we should make to God?

_____

_____

_____

_____

_____

CLOSING QUESTIONS

In what ways is Jesus a better king than Saul, David, and Solomon, even in their best days?

_____

_____

_____

_____

_____

_____

What central themes are developing in the storyline of the Bible so far?

_____

_____

_____

_____

_____

As you consider how you are a part of this ongoing story, how can seeing God's faithfulness in the past comfort or encourage you today?

_____

_____

_____

_____

_____

_____

Part 4

GOD'S KINGDOM DECLINED AND PARTIALLY RESTORED

God brings Israel to a high point during the reign of Solomon. He establishes Solomon's reign, gives him unmatched wisdom, and draws the nations to his rule. But Solomon turns from the Lord, and the people of Israel continue their centuries-long pattern of idolatry and disobedience. The united kingdom of Israel splits into northern and southern kingdoms. God uses the Assyrians to judge and exile the northern kingdom of Israel. Later he uses the Babylonians to judge and exile the southern kingdom of Judah. As God promised through Moses long before, he would remove his blessings from Israel if they continued in rebellious unbelief. Israel is exiled from their good land just as Adam and Eve were exiled from Eden in the beginning.

But God continues to remain faithful to his covenant promises to Abraham and to Israel and to David—promises that will lead ultimately to the restoration of God's presence and blessing to all nations. He raises up the Persian ruler Cyrus to conquer Babylon and send many Israelites back to their land. These Israelites raise a new temple and rebuild Jerusalem's walls. It is a day of small things—it certainly is not the full and glorious restored kingdom God promised through the prophets—but the Lord is blessing them. They now must trust him for a coming day of greater blessing, a day in which he will send his true King to restore Israel and send his blessings to the nations.

21. THE KINGDOM DIVIDED
1 Kings 11–14

Why is Solomon's idolatry (and all idolatry) such an offense to God, especially in light of God's lavish grace and blessings?

_____

_____

_____

_____

_____

Why is it such a turning point and tragedy for most of Israel to reject and split from the house of David, especially in light of God's kingdom promises to David and his descendants?

22. JUDAH EXILED

2 Kings 21–25

How are the primary institutions of Israel (i.e., temple, sacrifice, priesthood, the law, prophets) affected in this section?

How does the favorable treatment of King Jehoiachin at the end of this section provide hope for Israel's future?

_____

_____

_____

_____

_____

23. EXILES RETURN AND REBUILD THE TEMPLE
Ezra 1–3

Why is it so important for Israel to rebuild the temple (in light of what we know about the purposes of the tabernacle and the temple)?

_____

_____

_____

_____

What does this section teach us about God's faithfulness?

_____

_____

_____

_____

24. ISRAEL RECOMMITS TO OBEY GOD

Nehemiah 8–10

What do we learn about the importance of God's Word from the narrative of Ezra's reading and the people's response?

As the people confess their sin and recount their history, what themes do they highlight?

What does the content of this prayer teach us about God's character and the way he has acted throughout Israel's history?

_____

_____

_____

_____

_____

CLOSING QUESTIONS

What does the history of Israel teach about the problem of the human heart?

_____

_____

_____

_____

What have we learned about God's patience from the way in which he has related to Israel up to this point in Israel's story?

_____

_____

_____

_____

How might these reflections, together with what we have learned from Israel's prayer of confession, lead us to pray to the Lord differently?

Part 5

THE HOPE OF RESTORATION

Israel's story parallels that of Adam and Eve: each receives the blessing of God's presence, his good commands, and flourishing land but then rejects God and endures a judgment of exile from his presence. Throughout the period of Israel's decline, exile, and partial return, God sends prophets to warn of judgment and to promise a glorious future.

Through Isaiah God promises his exiled people a new and better exodus—one that will rescue them not merely from bondage in Babylon but from the bondage of sin and death. And God promises that he will do so through a true and ideal Israelite, a true and better servant of the Lord. This servant will live the faithful life that Israel (and each of us) fails to live, die as an offering for sin, and rise again to spread God's blessing. This new exodus through the true servant will bring about a new creation—a renewed world for all who repent and believe.

Jeremiah adds to this hope the promise of a new covenant, by which all God's people will experience full forgiveness, transformed hearts, and permanent relationship with him. And through Ezekiel God promises to shepherd his people through a true and better Davidic king and to raise his people from the dead.

All of these promises will begin to be fulfilled with the coming of Jesus, but Israel receives them in hope.

25. THE HOPE OF A NEW EXODUS
Isaiah 52–55

What are the key aspects of who the Lord's servant is and what he accomplishes?

_____

_____

_____

_____

_____

What do you know about Jesus that makes it clear he fulfills the role of this servant?

_____

_____

_____

_____

_____

How does this section make clear that the salvation the servant provides is utterly gracious and free for even the worst sinners who receive it?

_____

_____

_____

_____

_____

_____

26. THE HOPE OF A NEW CREATION

Isaiah 63–66

How does this text demonstrate our eternal future in a real, physical, renewed creation?

_____

_____

_____

_____

_____

_____

What encourages you most about this vision of the eternal future for God's people?

_____

_____

_____

_____

_____

What would it look like to cultivate a posture of one who is "humble and contrite in spirit and trembles at [God's] word"?

_____

_____

_____

_____

_____

_____

27. THE HOPE OF A NEW COVENANT

Jeremiah 30–33

What key promises of the new covenant does God give to his people?

_____

_____

_____

How do these promises solve the fundamental problem of Israel, as seen throughout their history?

How do we see that these promises have begun to be fulfilled and experienced by Christians today?

28. THE HOPE OF NEW LIFE

Ezekiel 34–37

How does the image of a shepherd in this section reveal God's character and commitment?

_____

_____

_____

_____

_____

How does Jesus fulfill the expectations both of (1) God's coming himself as a shepherd and (2) his sending a new Davidic king to shepherd his people?

_____

_____

_____

_____

_____

CLOSING QUESTIONS

What promises are most encouraging to you from these readings?

How does this section clarify and fill out your understanding of who
Jesus is and what he came to do?

What are you learning about the coherence of the story of Scripture,
with its unified storyline and developing themes, and how might this
strengthen your conviction of the divine origin of Scripture?

Part 6

THE DAWNING OF
THE KINGDOM

The Gospel of Mark shows Jesus' coming as the long-awaited
Savior and King. He announces, "The time is fulfilled, and the
kingdom of God is at hand; repent and believe in the gospel." The
Old Testament promises a day in which the kingdom of God will
arrive, and with it the salvation of God's people and the restoration
of all things. Jesus' announcement of the gospel—the good news—
signals that he is bringing these ancient promises to fulfillment.
He is the promised true king who will accomplish the new exodus,
inaugurate the new covenant, and launch the new creation.

Wherever Jesus goes, he uses his authority and Spirit to cause
the effects of the curse to flee: he casts out demons, heals people
from sickness and suffering, calms life-threatening storms. He
addresses mankind's root problem as he forgives sins. He teaches
his new people what it looks like to live as a renewed humanity: they
will be marked by humility and wholehearted devotion to God.

Jesus calls everyone to trust his word, follow him as their king, and suffer for his sake. He does not promise immediate freedom from all sin and suffering, but he does promise glory on the other side of those obstacles.

From the midpoint of the Gospel of Mark onward, Jesus sets his sights on Jerusalem. He knows that Jerusalem will be the place of his sacrifice, where he will fulfill Isaiah's ancient promise of the servant who would die for the sins of his people. But after doing so, Jesus rises again, signaling the dawn of the new creation. We are now all called to receive his gracious forgiveness, know him as our truest friend, and follow him as our king.

29. JESUS' MINISTRY BEGINS
Mark 1–4

How should we describe Jesus' purposes or mission in light of his words and actions in this section?

_____

_____

_____

_____

_____

_____

What do the four different soils represent in Jesus' parable?

How today do we still see each of these four responses to Jesus' word?

30. JESUS' MINISTRY CONTINUES
Mark 5–8

Where do we see Jesus' compassionate heart in action?

According to Jesus' teaching at the end of this section, what does it look like to follow him as a disciple?

_____

_____

_____

_____

_____

Why is following Jesus on the costly path of discipleship worth every sacrifice?

_____

_____

_____

_____

_____

31. JESUS' JOURNEY TO JERUSALEM
Mark 9–12

How does Jesus define greatness, and how is this in stark contrast to our culture's definition?

_____

_____

How would you summarize Jesus' teaching on what it means to follow him as a disciple?

How does Jesus' parable of the vineyard tenants retell the story of Israel?

32. JESUS' DEATH AND RESURRECTION
Mark 13–16

What is the main lesson for us from Jesus' teaching on the destruction of the temple and the persecution of his people?

How does Jesus' prayer in Gethsemane show his deep commitment to his Father and also to us?

In what various ways does Mark emphasize the historical reality of Jesus' death and resurrection?

_____

_____

_____

_____

CLOSING QUESTIONS

How has Mark's Gospel clarified your answer to the question of who Jesus is?

_____

_____

_____

_____

_____

_____

How does Jesus' death and resurrection accomplish salvation for all who trust him?

_____

_____

_____

_____

_____

What might you need to change in your life in light of Jesus' teaching on what it means to follow him?

_____

_____

_____

_____

_____

Part 7

THE GOSPEL SPREADS
AND ALL IS MADE NEW

The good news of Jesus creates an explosion of joy. People learn that they are part of a bigger story—that the God who made them reconciles them to himself on terms of grace.

The book of Acts begins with Jesus' commissioning of his apostles to be his "witnesses in Jerusalem and in all Judea and Samaria, and to the end of the earth." This order reflects God's promises to Abraham and the prophets: God would first restore believing Israelites and then spread his blessing through them to the ends of the earth. Acts shows how Christians carry the message of Jesus to the ends of the earth in the power of the Spirit. One of the greatest missionaries is the apostle Paul—he spreads the gospel, makes disciples, and plants many churches. He also writes letters such as Ephesians to show how the good news of Jesus must transform every part of our lives.

Revelation culminates the Bible with a symbolic vision of Jesus and his sovereign rule over history. Jesus encourages his churches to maintain their first love and persevere in a hostile culture.

This message concludes with a beautiful picture of our eternal future. We will not live disembodied forever; we will live in a new creation with Jesus and his people. These final chapters tie together many of the themes that began in the first chapters of the Bible. God is our temple; the world is our Eden; Jesus is our sacrificial Lamb. All who trust in Jesus will be restored to reflect God's image by reigning with Jesus over all things forever.

33. THE CHURCH'S MISSION BEGINS
Acts 1–4

What key points about Jesus does Peter announce in his sermon at Pentecost?

In Peter's speech in Solomon's Portico, what key expectations from the Old Testament does he mention as being fulfilled through Jesus?

In what ways can we see the Holy Spirit present and working in the early church?

34. THE CHURCH MULTIPLIES IN JERUSALEM AND BEYOND

Acts 5–8

Why were the early Christians able to rejoice even in the midst of great suffering?

How did God use great challenges or persecution to spread the gospel and multiply the church?

35. THE GOSPEL BEGINS TO SPREAD TO THE GENTILES
Acts 9–12

What does Paul's conversion story teach us about the grace, compassion, and power of Jesus?

What is the main lesson God teaches Peter through his vision and visit with Cornelius?

How can God's grace to Paul and to Cornelius's family give hope to even the most rebellious of sinners?

36. THE GOSPEL CONTINUES TO SPREAD
Acts 13–15

In Paul's speech at Antioch in Pisidia, how does he root his proclamation about Jesus in the Old Testament story?

Why was it so important for Paul to return to his church plants in order to teach and strengthen them?

_____

_____

_____

_____

_____

What does the Jerusalem Council conclude about whether people must not only believe the gospel but also be circumcised in order to be saved? Why?

_____

_____

_____

_____

_____

37. THE GOSPEL EXPLAINED
Ephesians 1–3

What are the spiritual blessings that Paul celebrates and declares that every Christian possesses because of God's grace in Christ?

_____

_____

_____

_____

_____

_____

To what aspects of God's character does Paul draw attention as he reflects on why God "made us alive together with Christ"?

_____

_____

_____

_____

_____

What is Paul's overall tone as he reflects on how God "made us alive," and how should this shape our overall tone in life?

_____

_____

_____

_____

_____

38. THE GOSPEL APPLIED

Ephesians 4–6

What key virtues does Paul emphasize first, and in what ways are these needed today?

_____

_____

_____

_____

_____

What difference does it make to know that we obey not in order to receive Christ's love and acceptance but because we already have these gifts?

_____

_____

_____

_____

_____

How should the gospel transform and shape relationships between Christians?

_____

_____

_____

39. THE KING SPEAKS TO HIS CHURCHES

Revelation 1–3

What overall impression should this symbolic, Old Testament–image-laden vision of Christ make on us as readers?

What are a few of the key emphases of Jesus' messages to his seven churches?

40. THE RETURN OF THE KING AND THE RESTORATION OF ALL THINGS

Revelation 19–22

How should the reality of the coming judgment change how we view our lives today?

_____

_____

_____

_____

_____

In comparing the Bible's end with its beginning, what similarities and differences do you see?

_____

_____

_____

_____

_____

What biblical themes do you see coming to their ultimate fulfillment in this description of our eternal future?

_____

_____

_____

_____

_____

_____

CLOSING QUESTIONS

What do we learn about the character and heart of God from reflecting on the gospel and how he saves us?

_____

_____

_____

_____

_____

How would your life change if you took the truths you learned here more seriously—if they became alive and operative in your deepest self?

_____

_____

_____

_____

What difference would it make if God and this hopeful vision of our eternal future were on our minds more often?

_____

_____

_____

_____

_____

NOTES